Sólo Animales
(Only Animals)

Luciano Trigos

WetDog

Sólo Animales
(Only Animals)

Luciano Trigos

Paintings by Luciano Trigos
Layout & Cover: WetDog

Pintura de Luciano Trigos
Maqueta y portada: WetDog

ISBN: 9798355568467

www.hemoficcion.com/luciano-trigos-pintura
opensea.io/LucianoTrigos
opensea.io/Wet-Dog

All Rights reserved, including de right of reproducción in whole or in part in any form.

Copyright © 2022 Luciano Trigos

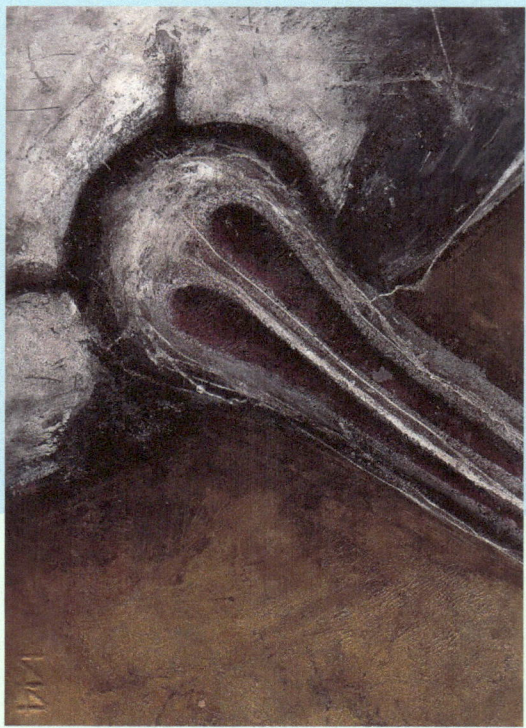

GLOSSARY (*Glosario*)

Mixed technique	Técnica mixta
Enamel	Esmalte sintético
Canvas	Tela / Lienzo
Oil	Óleo
Cardboard	Cartulina
Acrylic	Acrílico
Woodcut	Xilografía
Earth Worms	Lombrices
Hemofiction	Hemoficción
DAC	Dynamic Abstract Chromatics

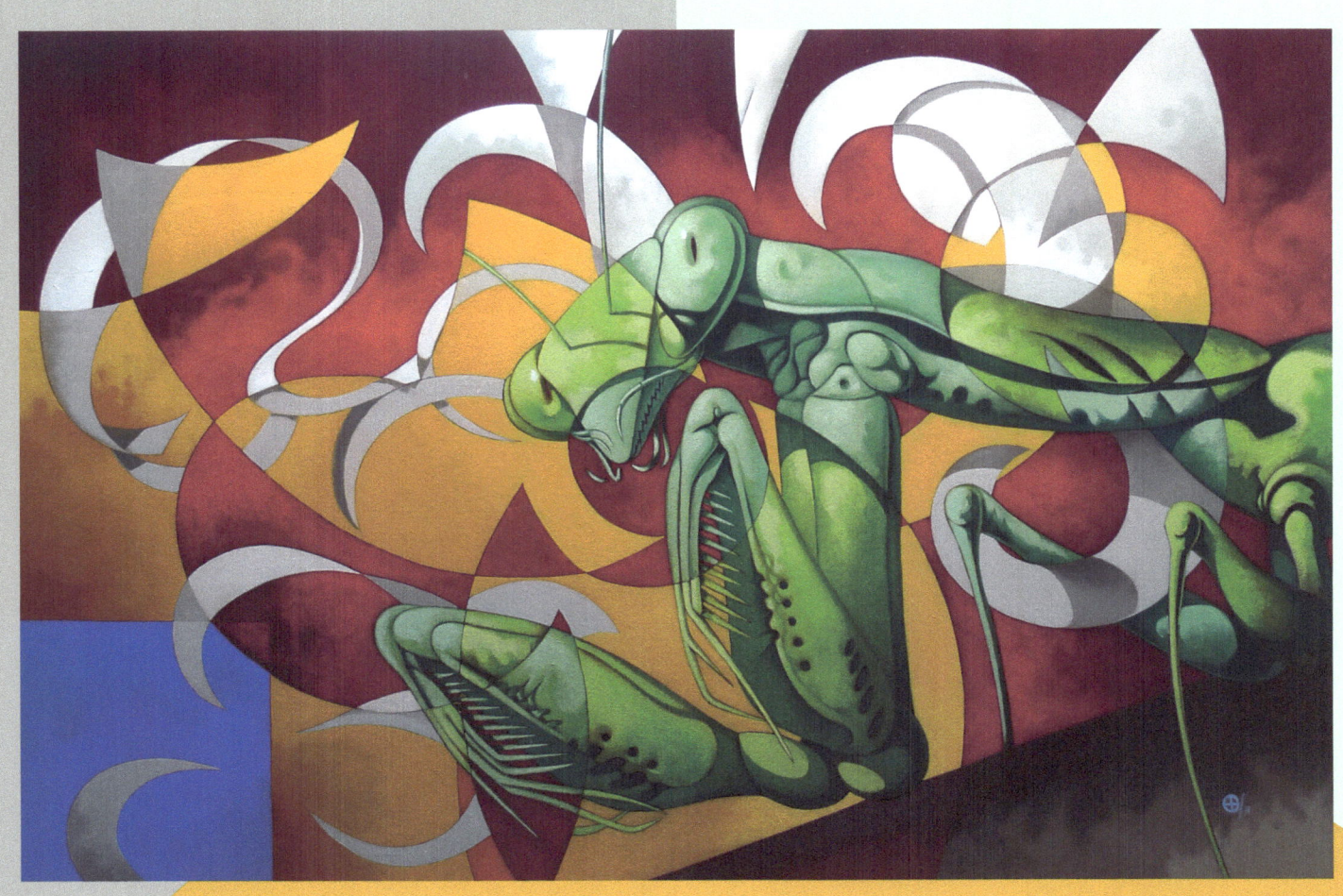

Hemofiction in ambush
Enamel / Canvas
24" X 36"
2011

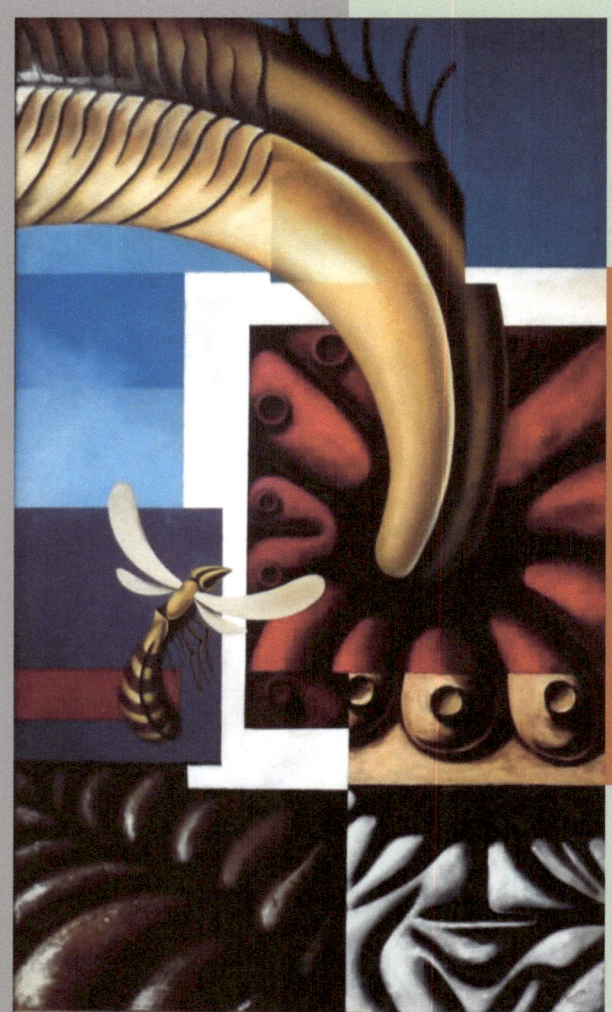

Onirismo carnal
Mixed technique / Canvas
120 cm X 80 cm
1995

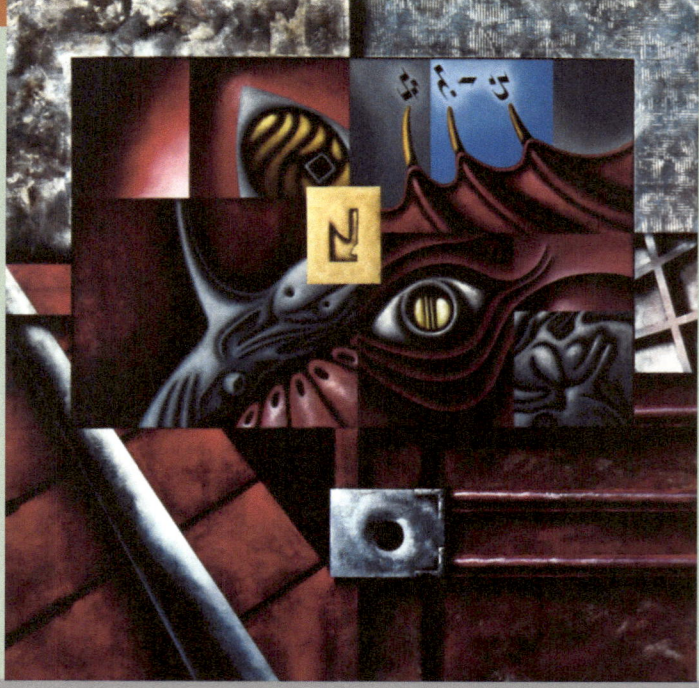

Insecto
Mixed technique / Wood & Canvas
150 cm X 150 cm
1997

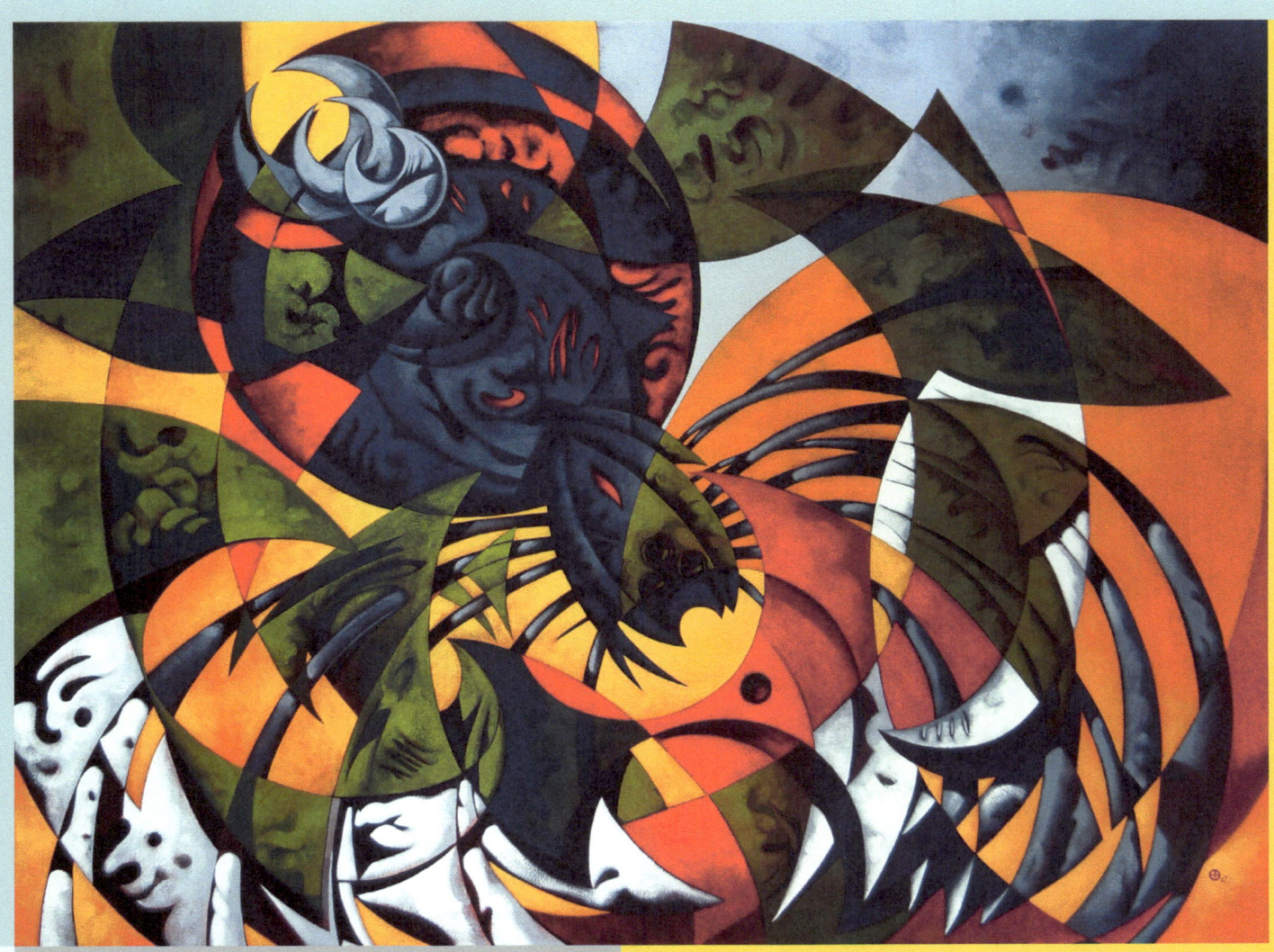

Hemofiction spider
Enamel / Canvas
36" X 48"
2007

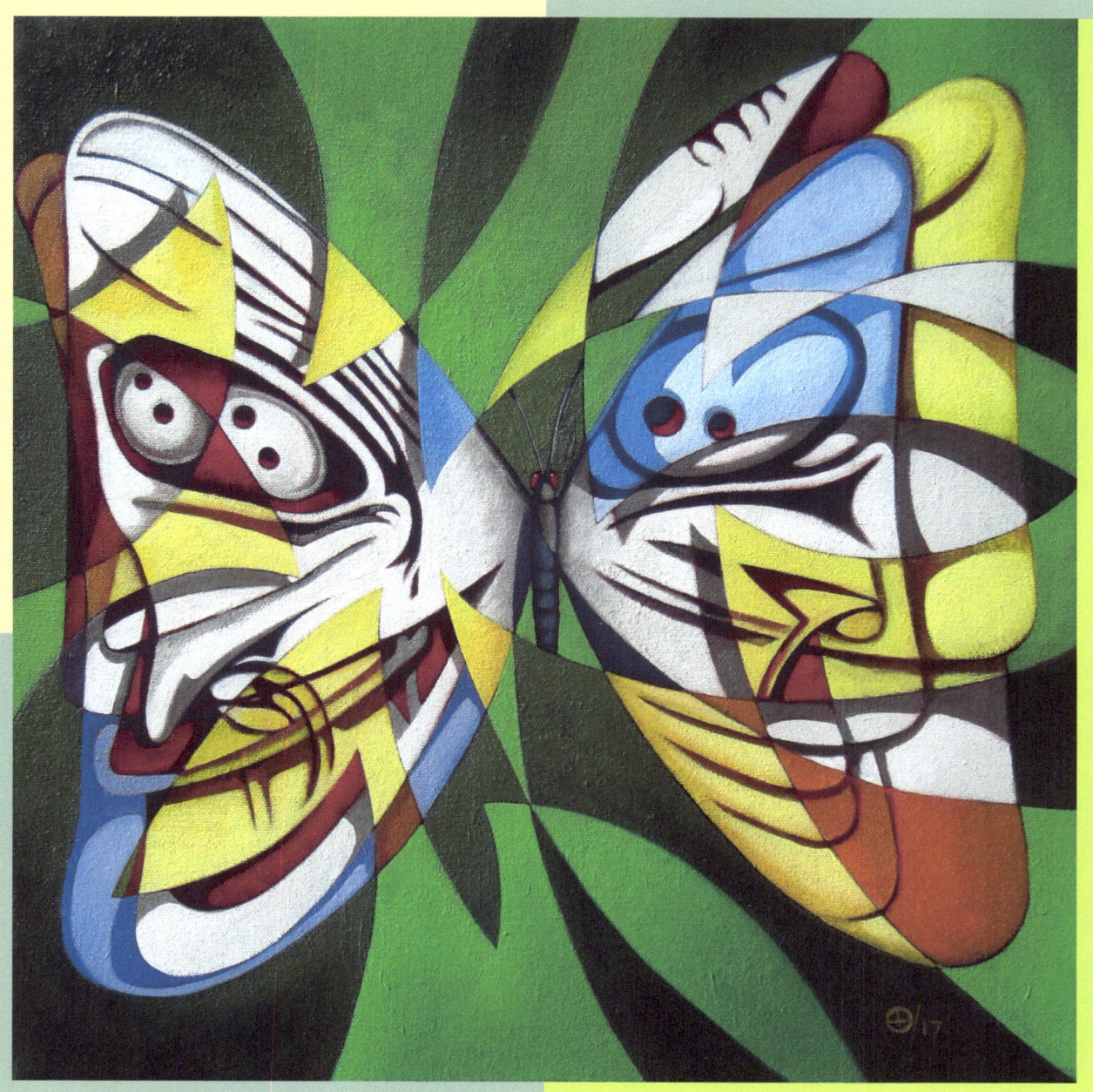

Polilla seductora
Oil / Canvas
40 cm x 40 cm
2017

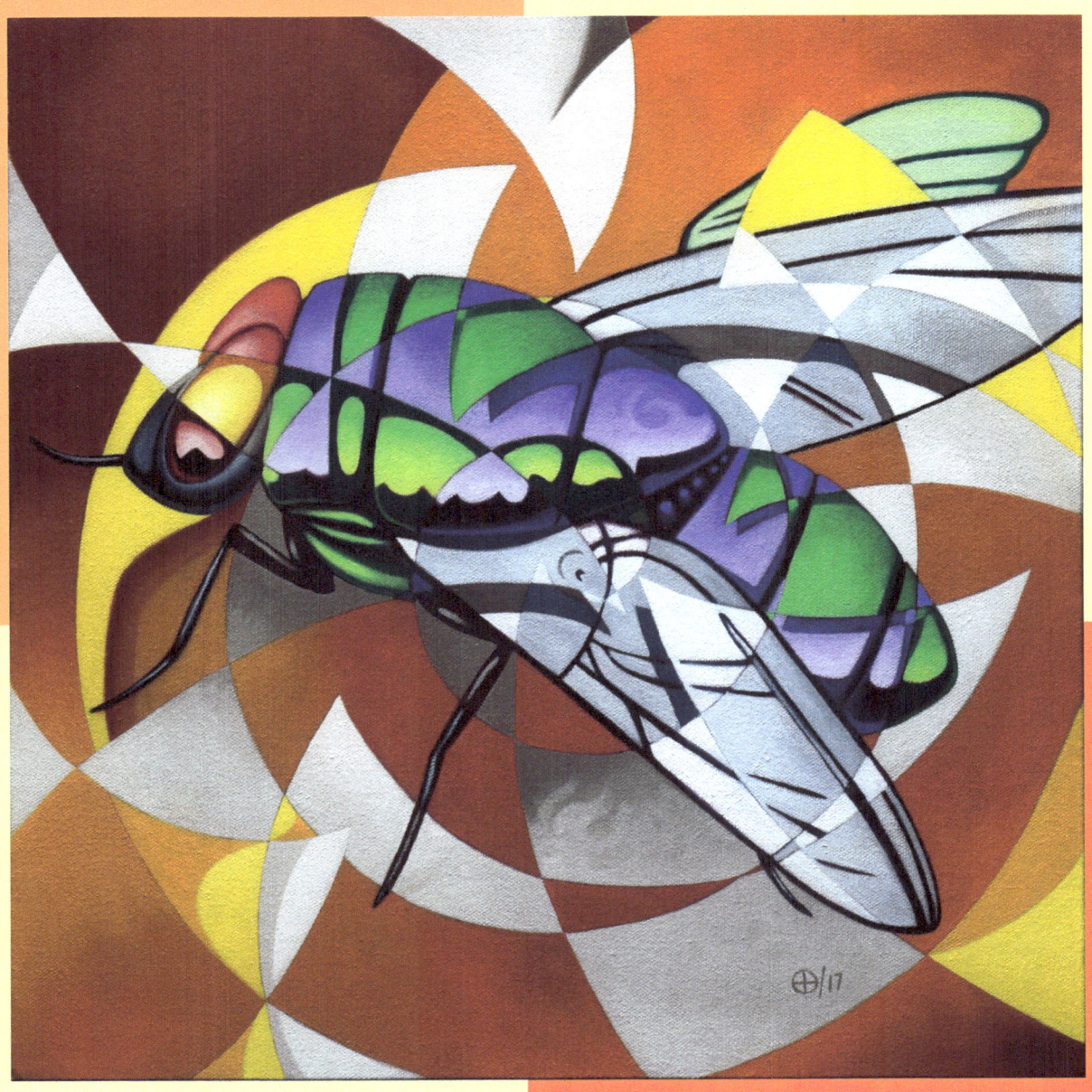

Mosca en mosca
Oil / Canvas
40 cm x 40 cm
2017

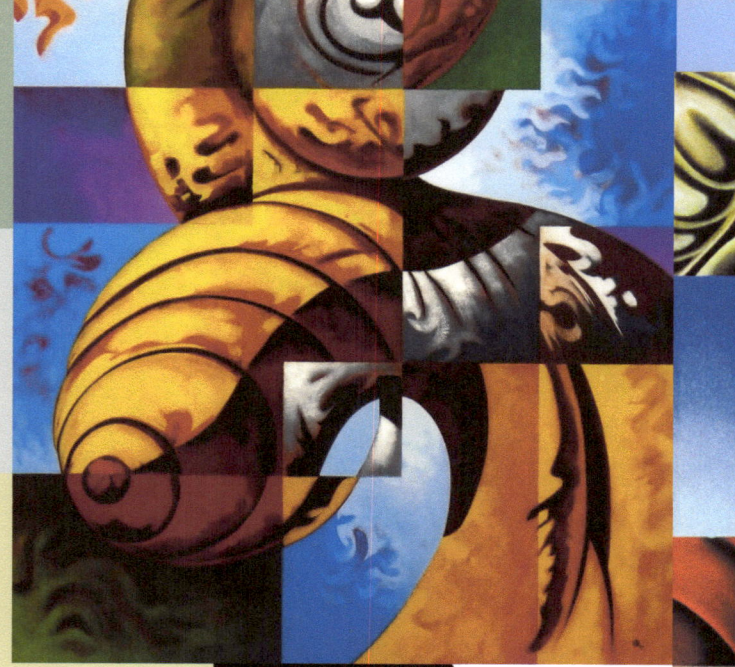

DAC 31
Enamel / Canvas
48" x 36"

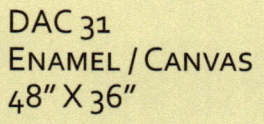

DAC 31
Woodcut
17 cm x 14 cm

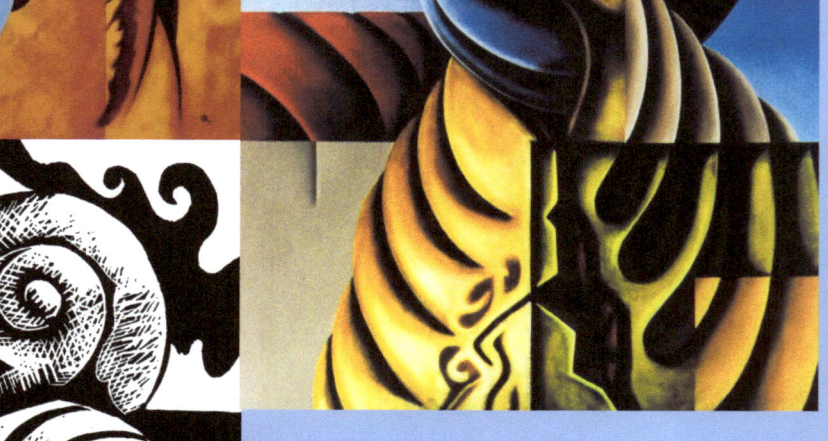

Carnada estética
Oil / Canvas
120 cm x 80 cm

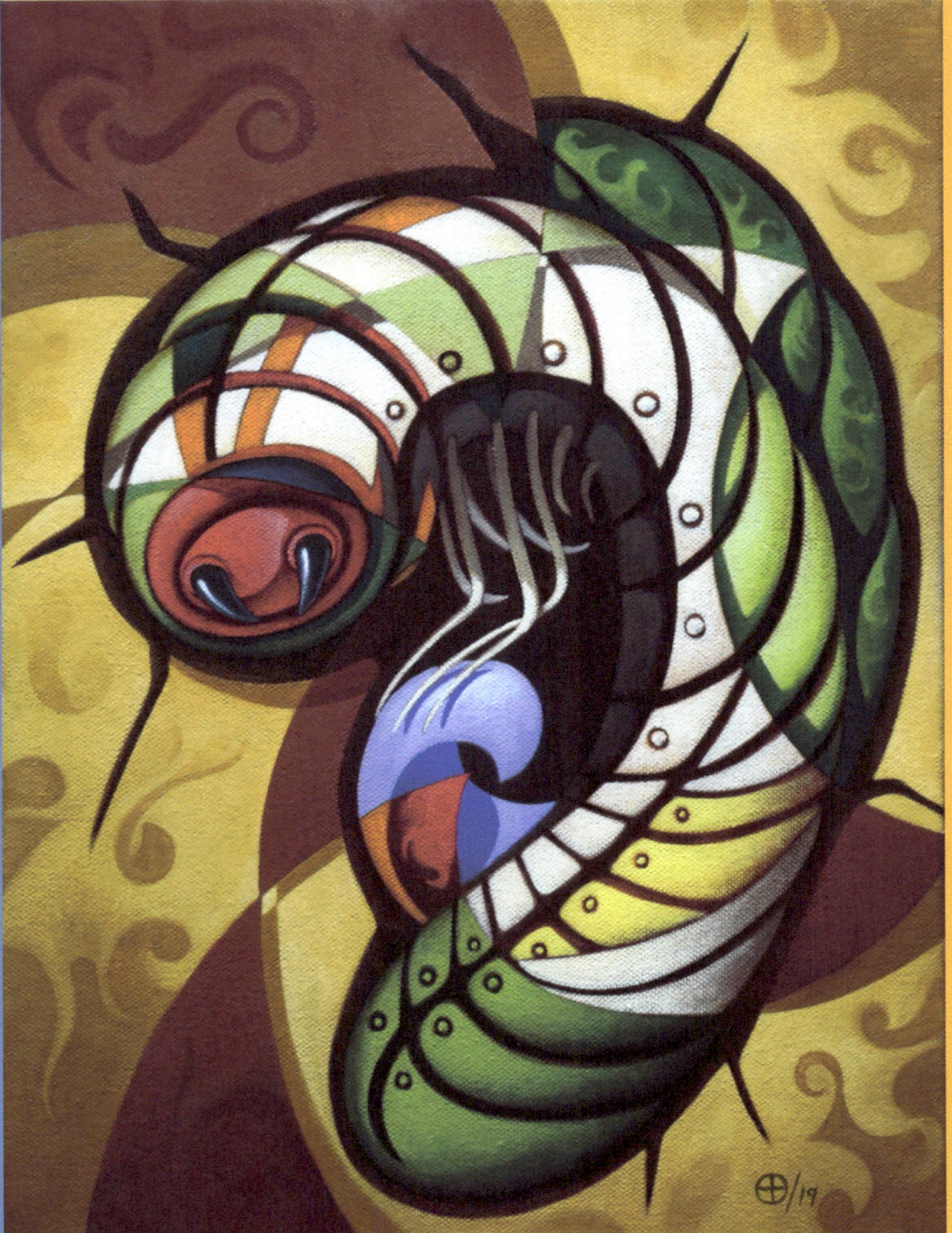

Cadencias de gusano
Oil / Canvas
40 cm x 30 cm
2019

9

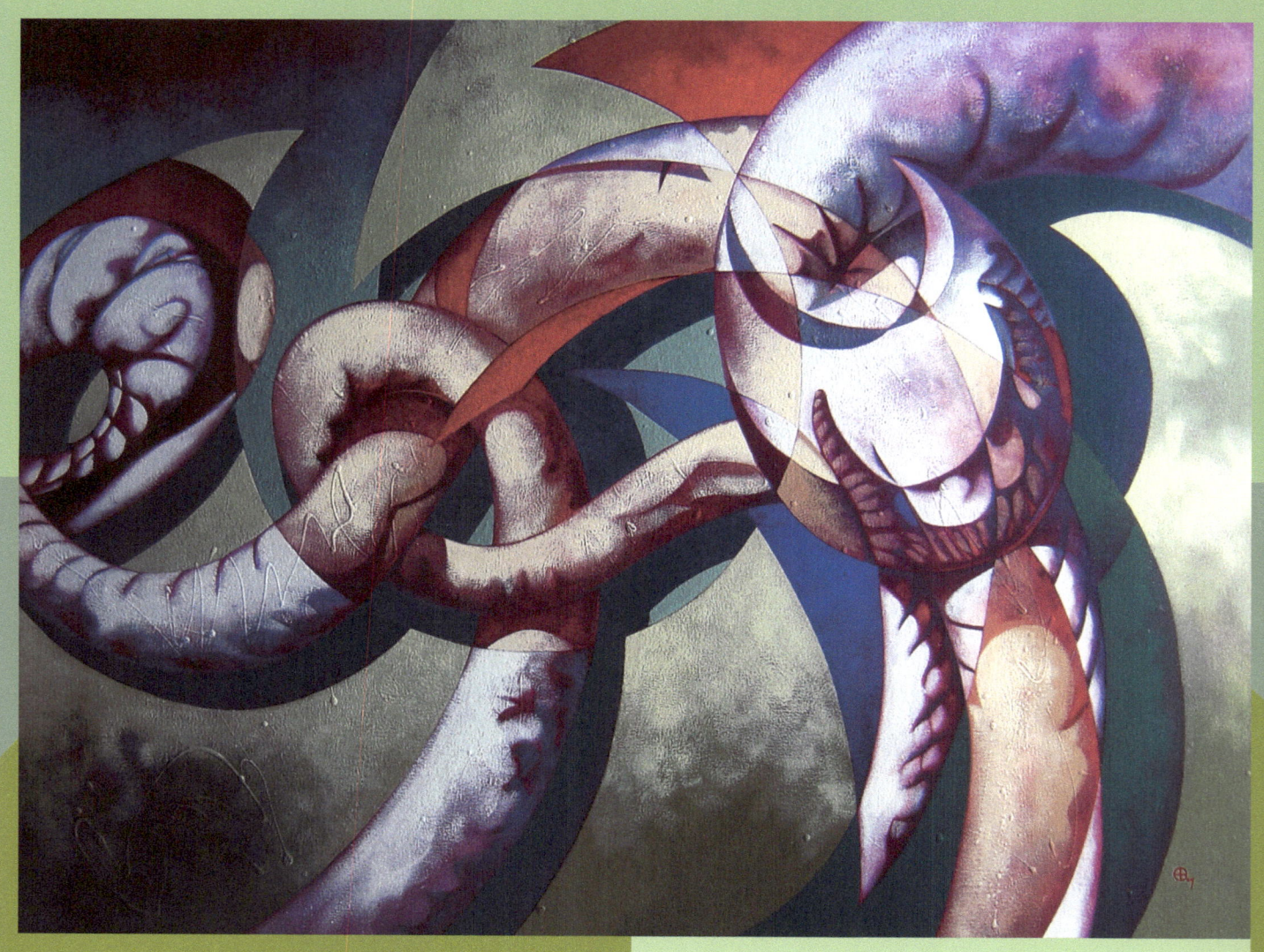

Earth worms
Enamel / Canvas
36" x 48"
2009

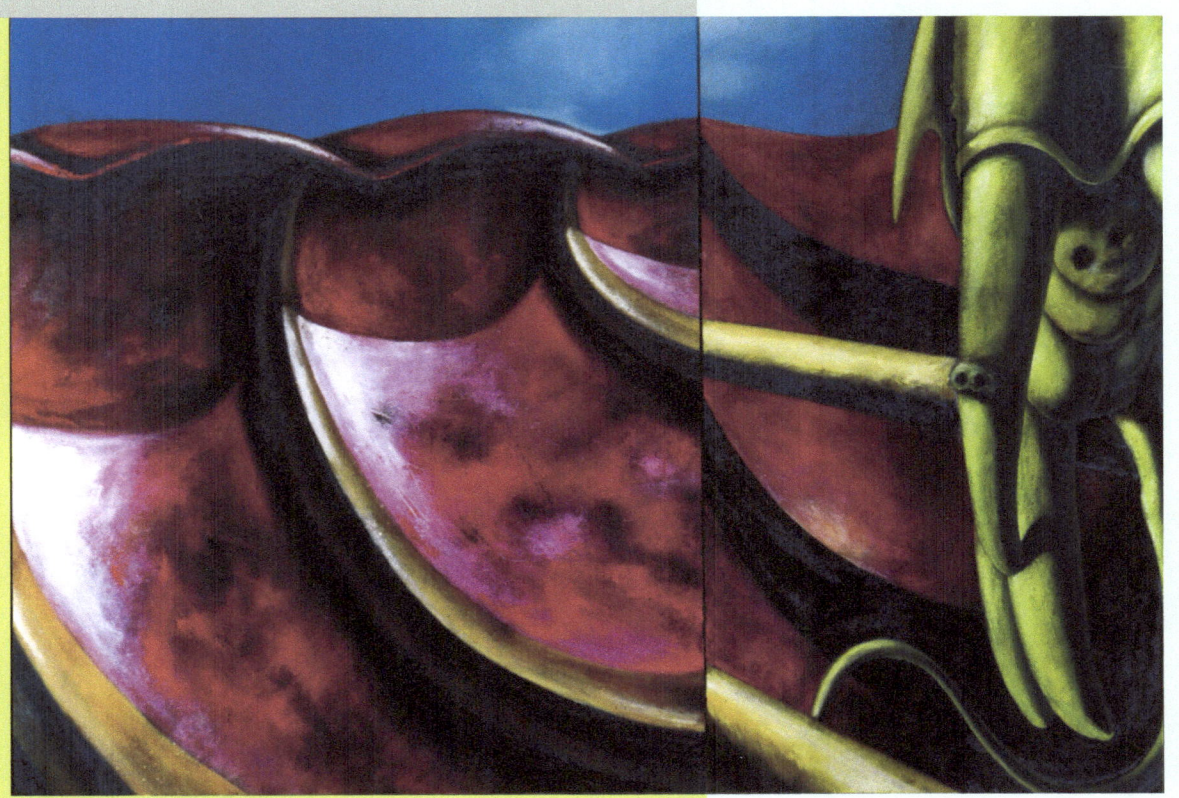

ÁCARO CON COSTILLA
OIL / CANVAS
120 CM X 200 CM
1993

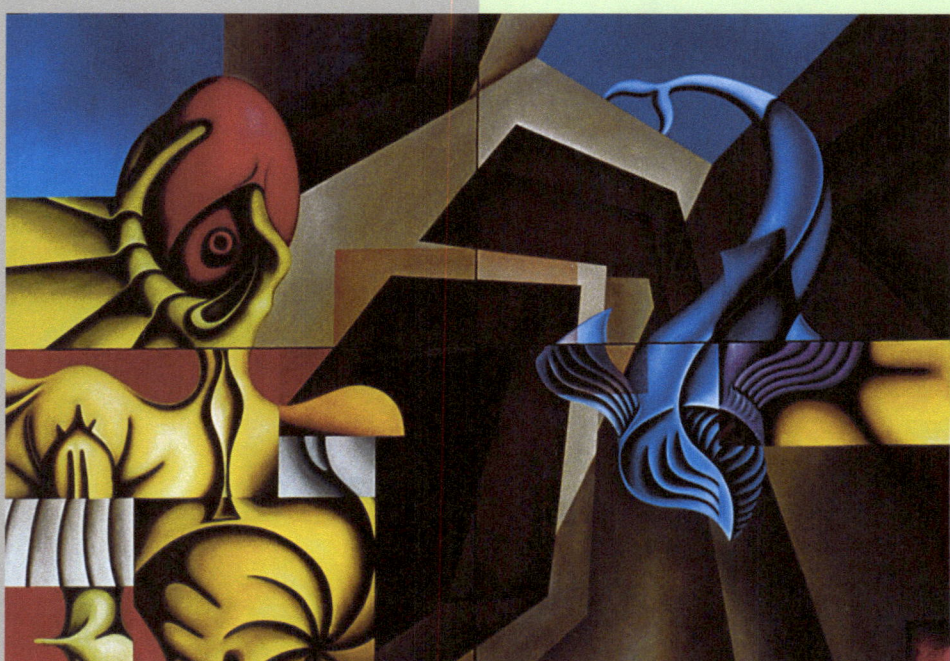

Reconversión IV
Oil / Canvas
200 cm x 240 cm
1990

Pez sin ojos
air brush / Cardboard
72 cm x 69 cm
1989

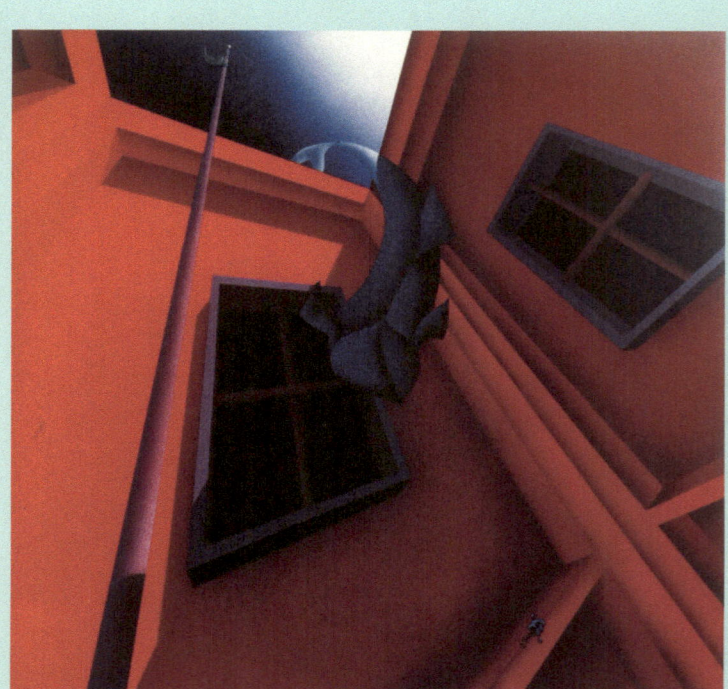

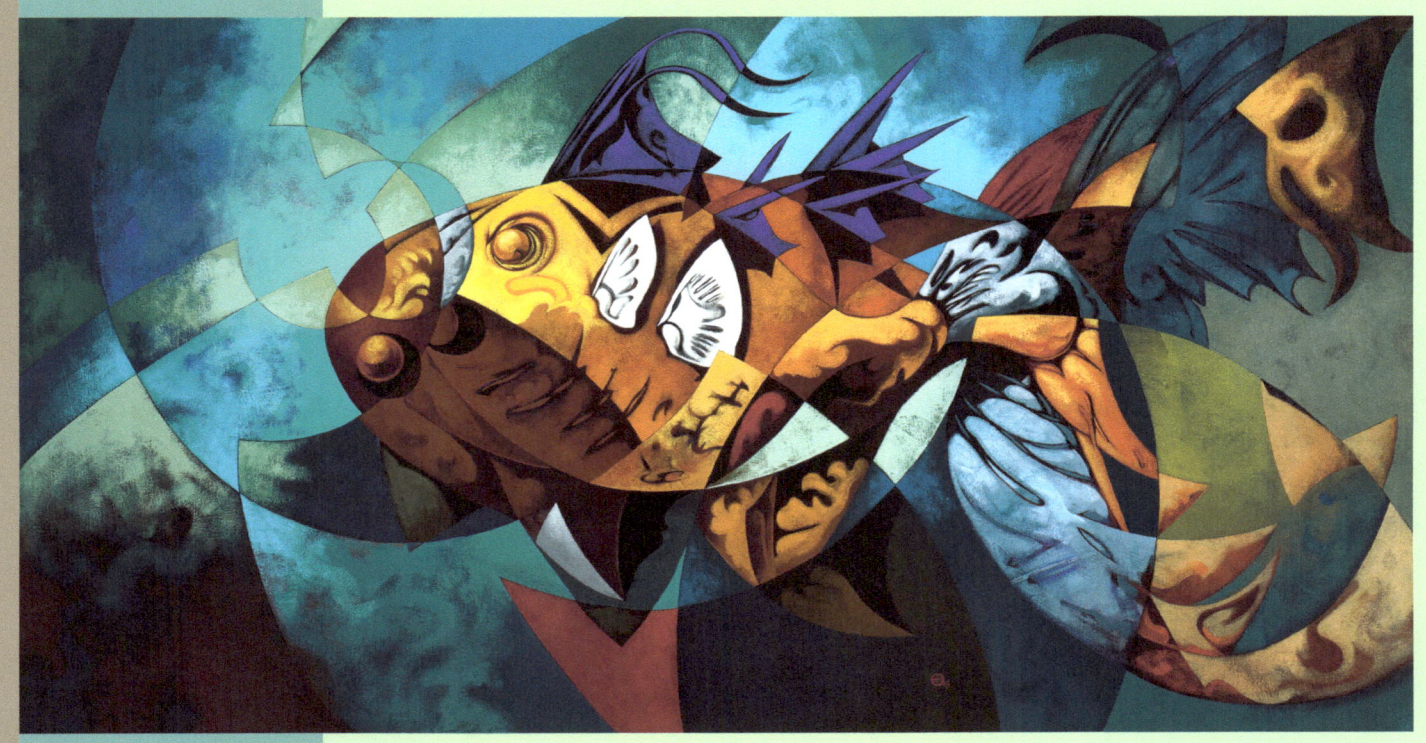

Hemofiction fish
Enamel / Canvas
31.5" X 60"
2005

13

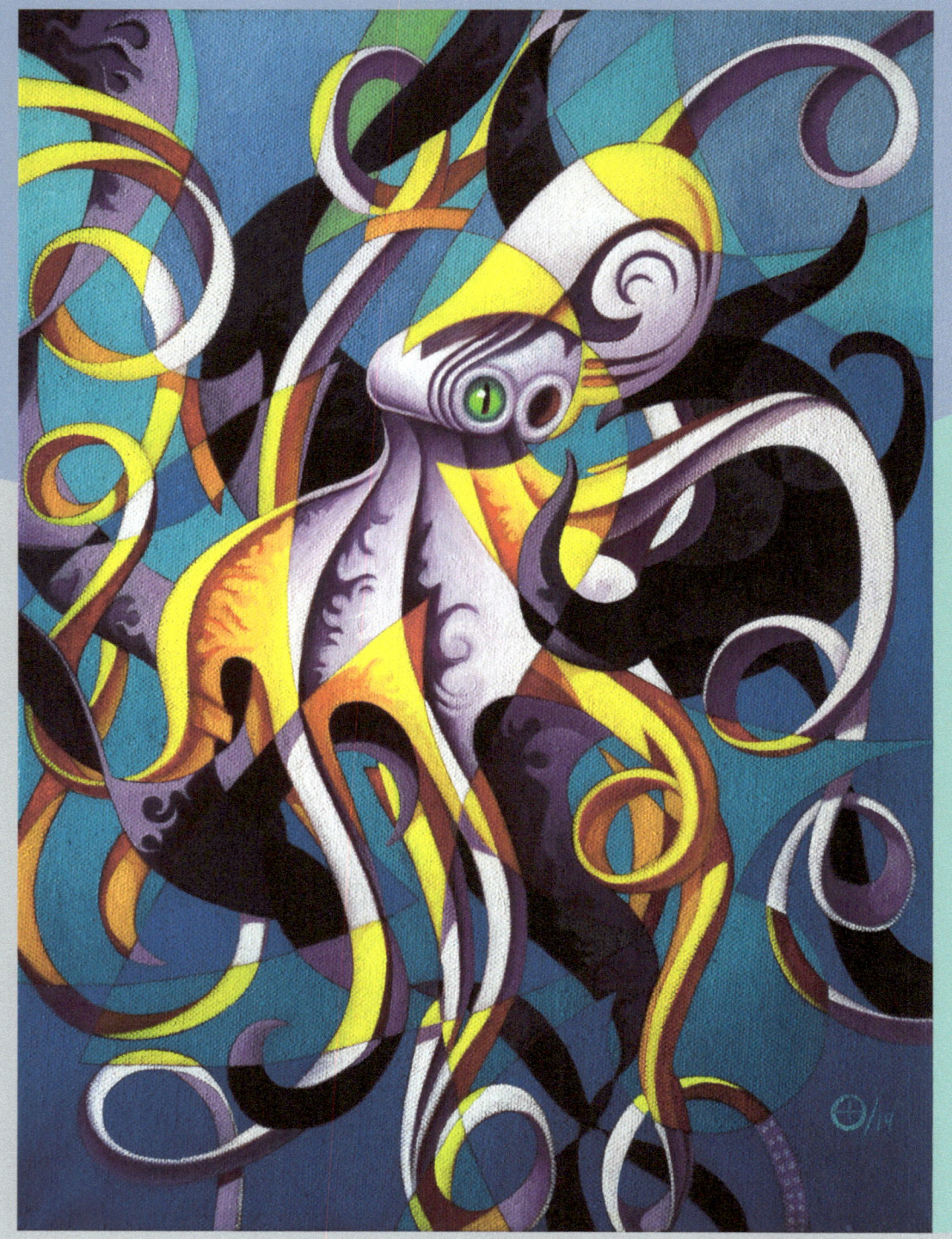

Pulpo exaltado
Oil / Canvas
40 cm x 30 cm
2019

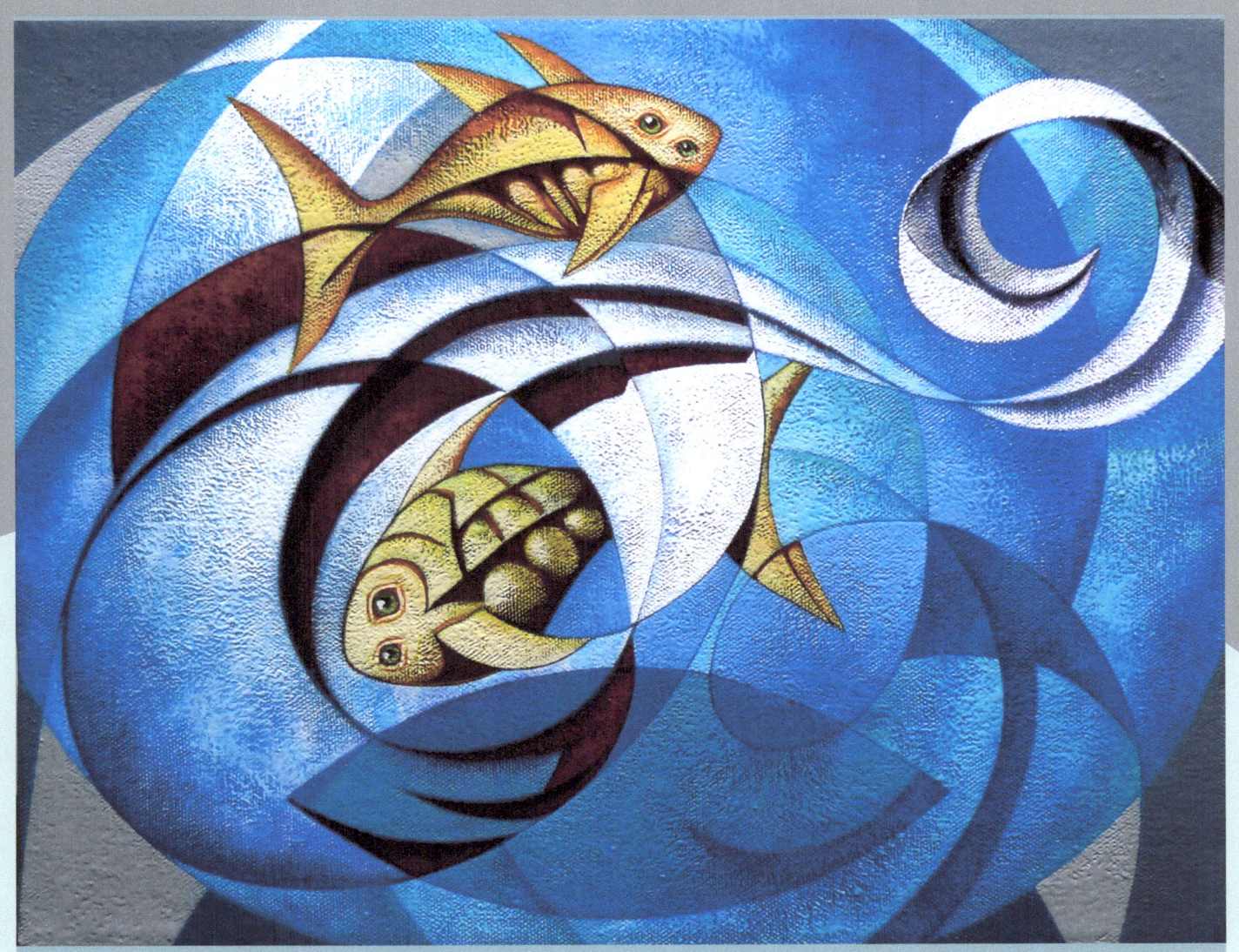

Fish bowl
Enamel / Canvas
11" x 14"
2010

15

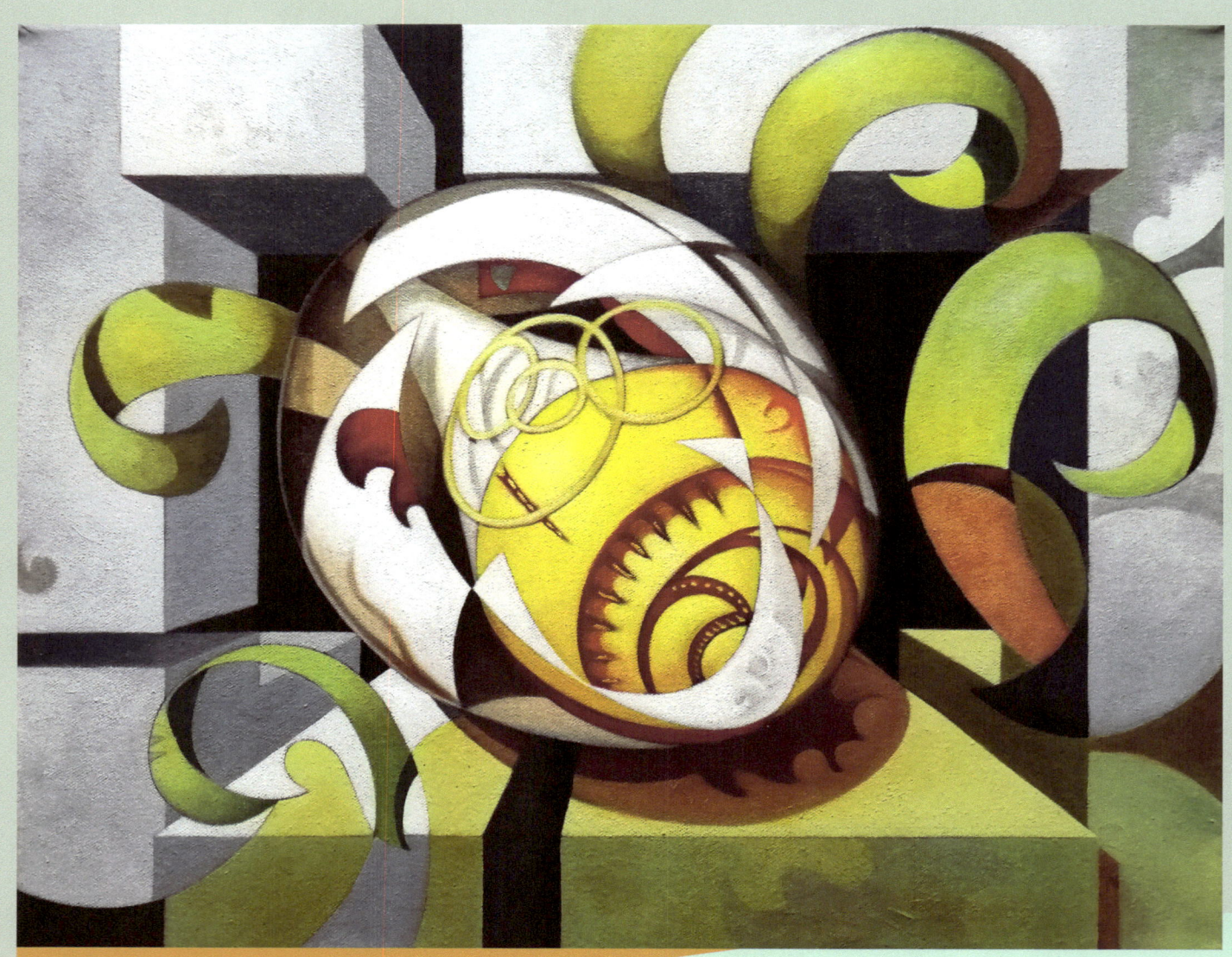

Uovo
Oil / Canvas
16" X 20"
2021

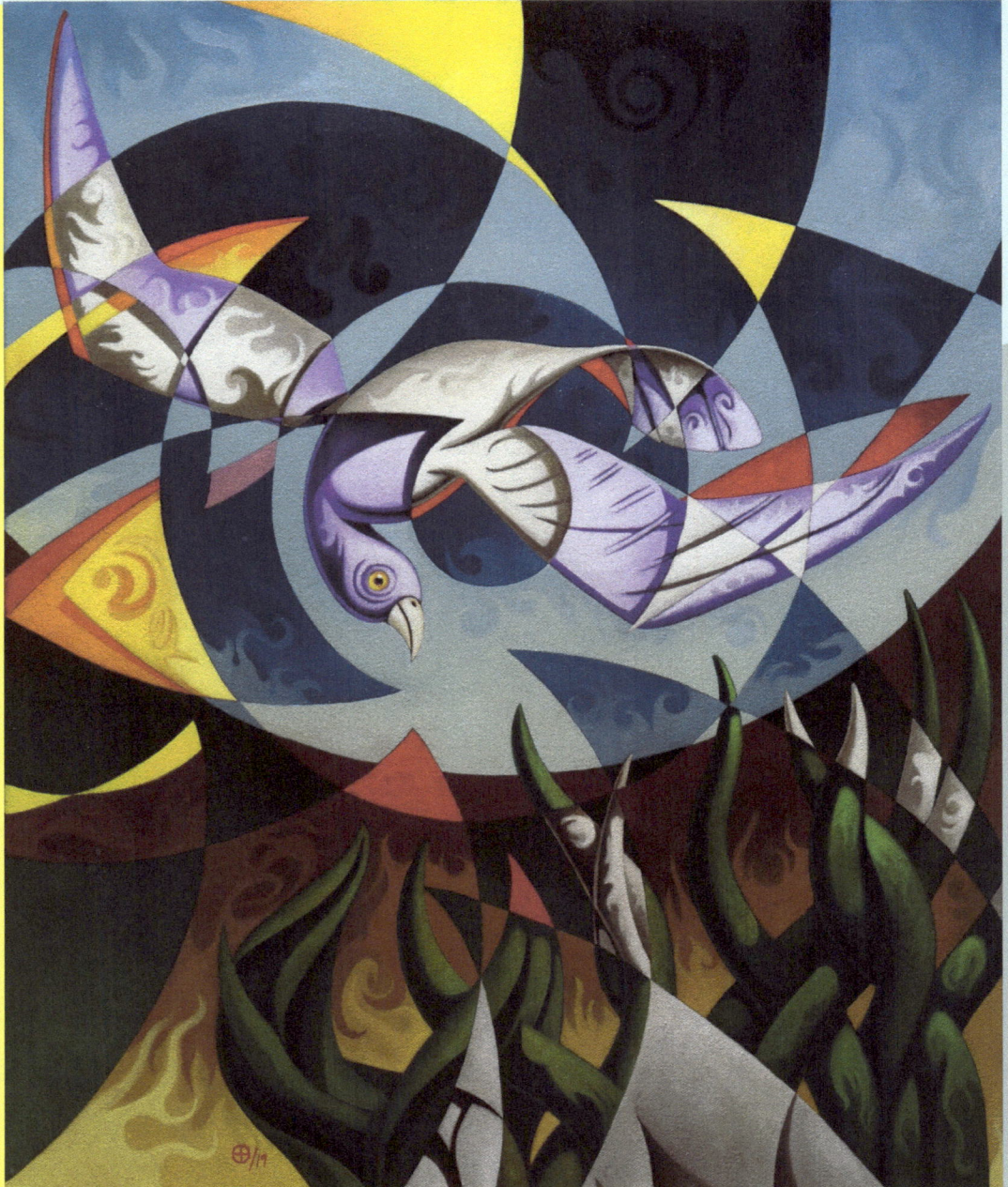

Paloma colateral
Oil / Canvas
60 cm x 50 cm
2019

17

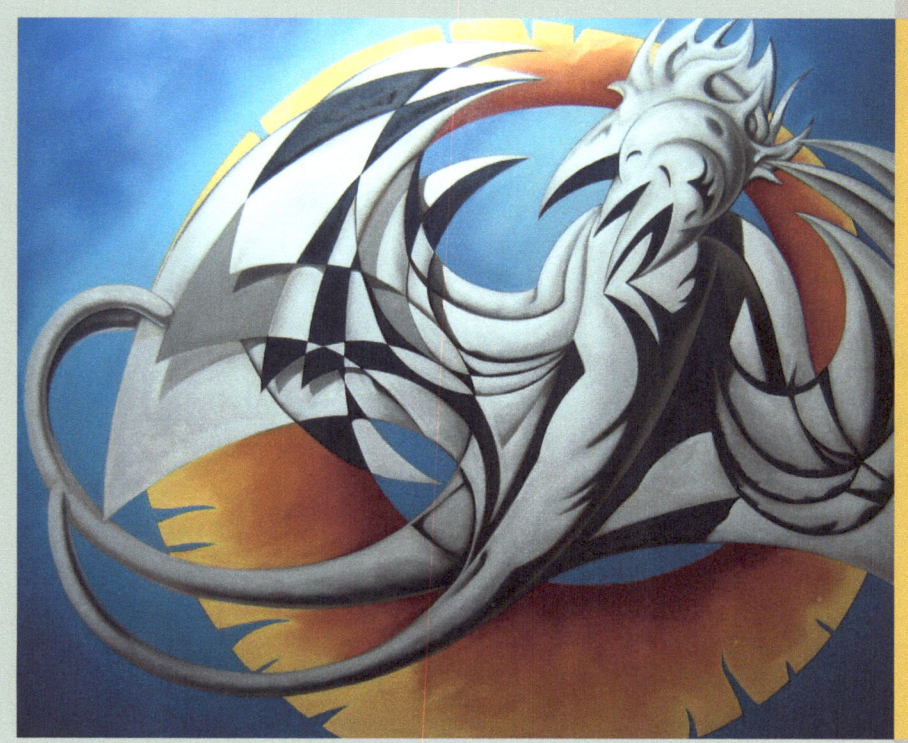

Ave iluminada
Oil / Canvas
100 cm x 120 cm
2008

Ave iluminada
Oil / Canvas
60 cm x 60 cm
2017

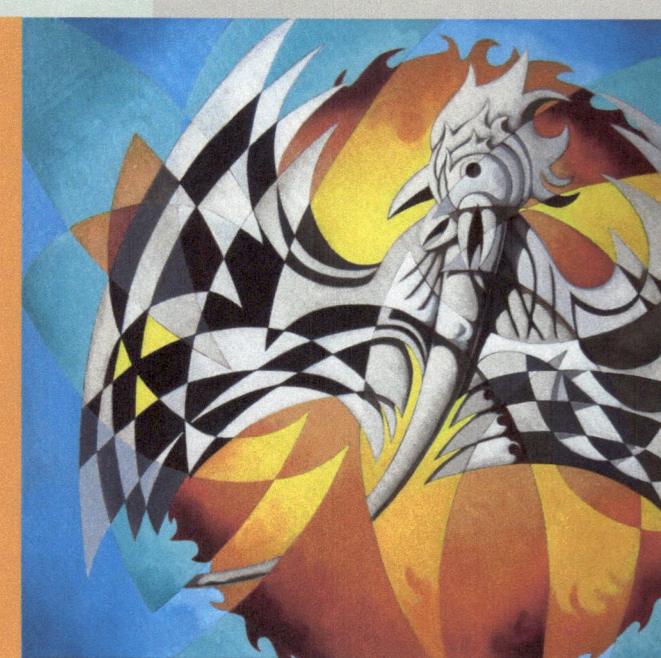

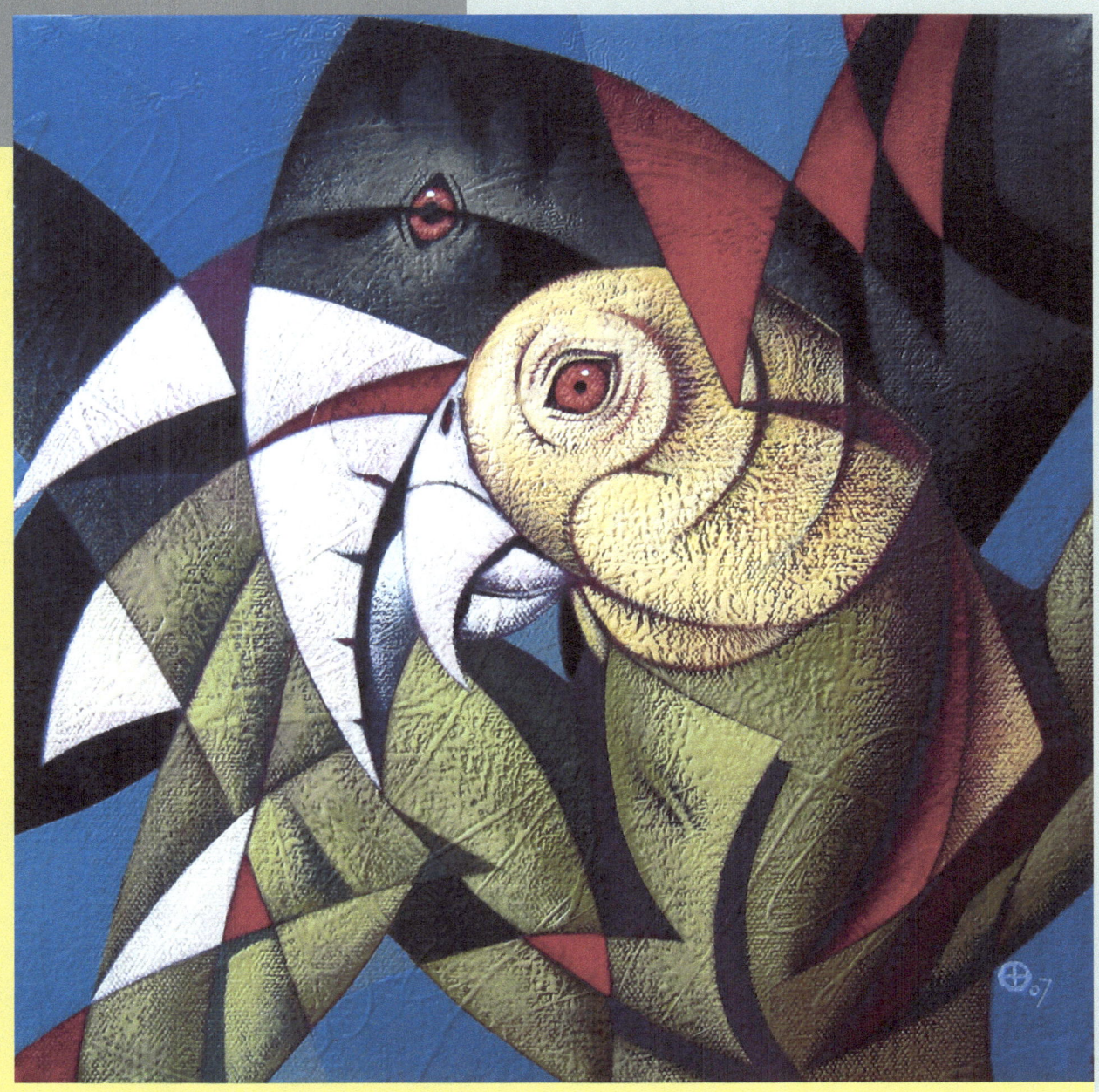

Hemofiction birds
Enamel / Canvas
10" X 10"
2007

19

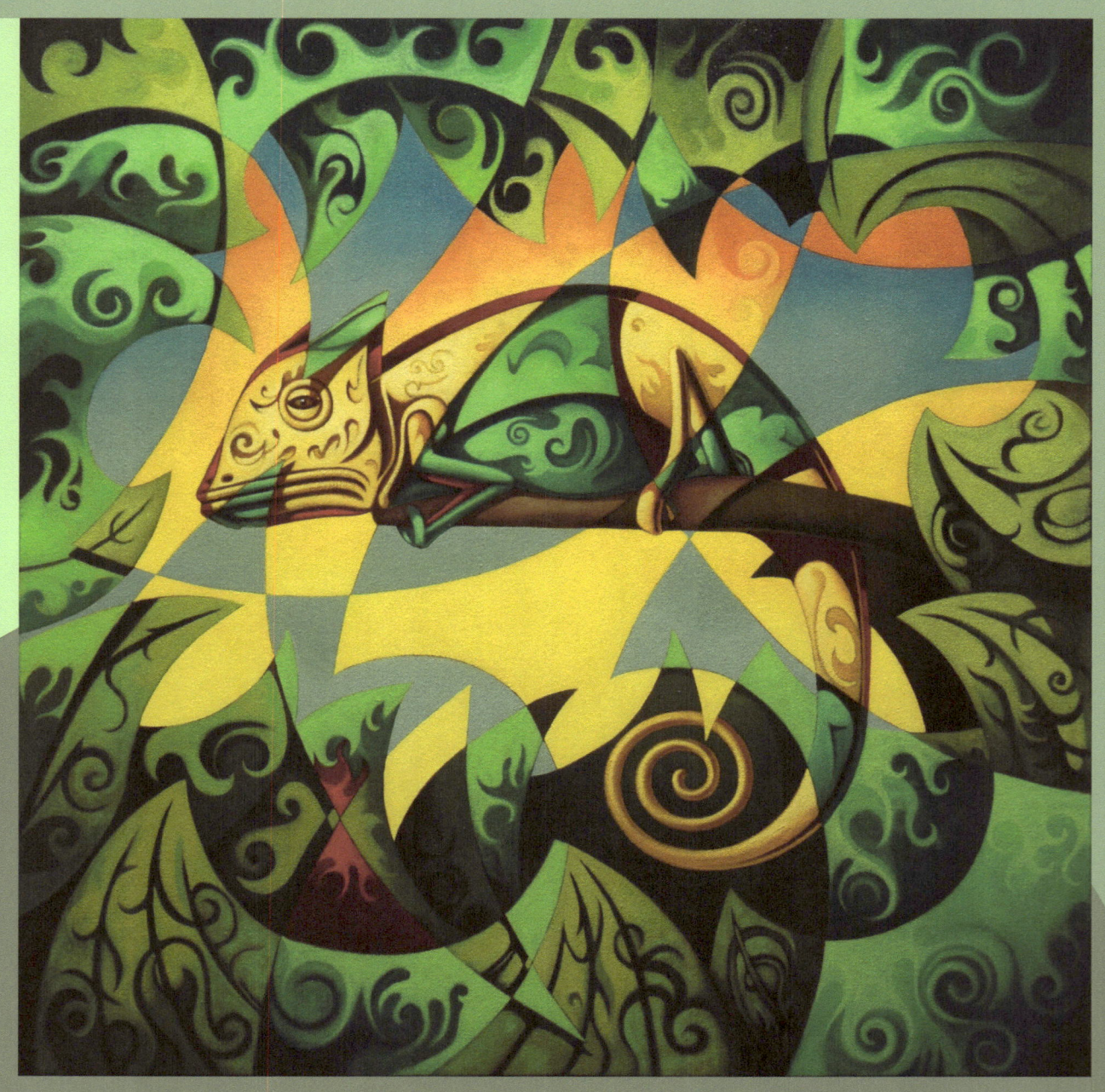

Remembranzas de lagartija
Oil / Canvas
60 cm x 60 cm
2019

20

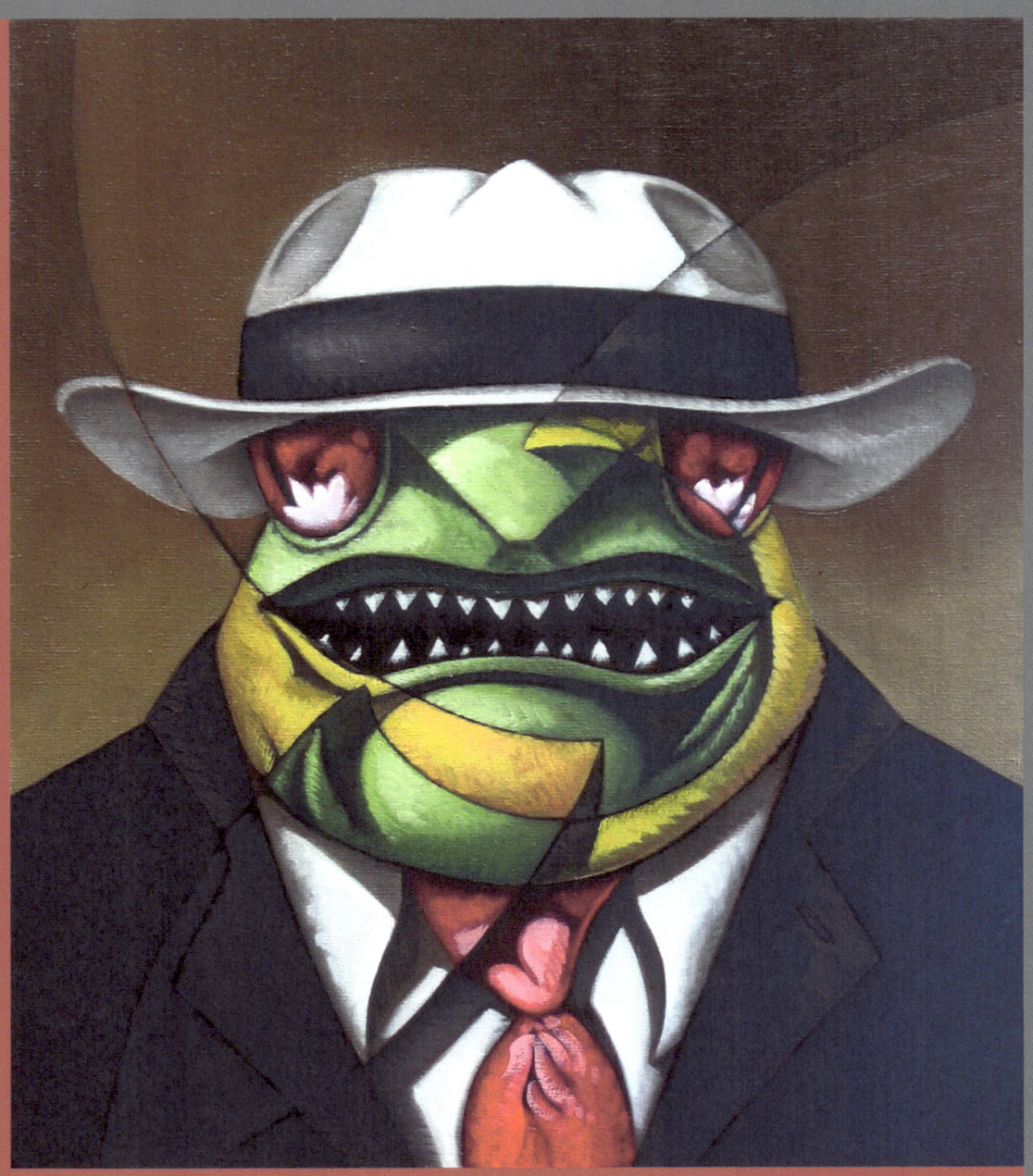

Sapo maton
Oil / Canvas
25 cm x20 cm
2008

21

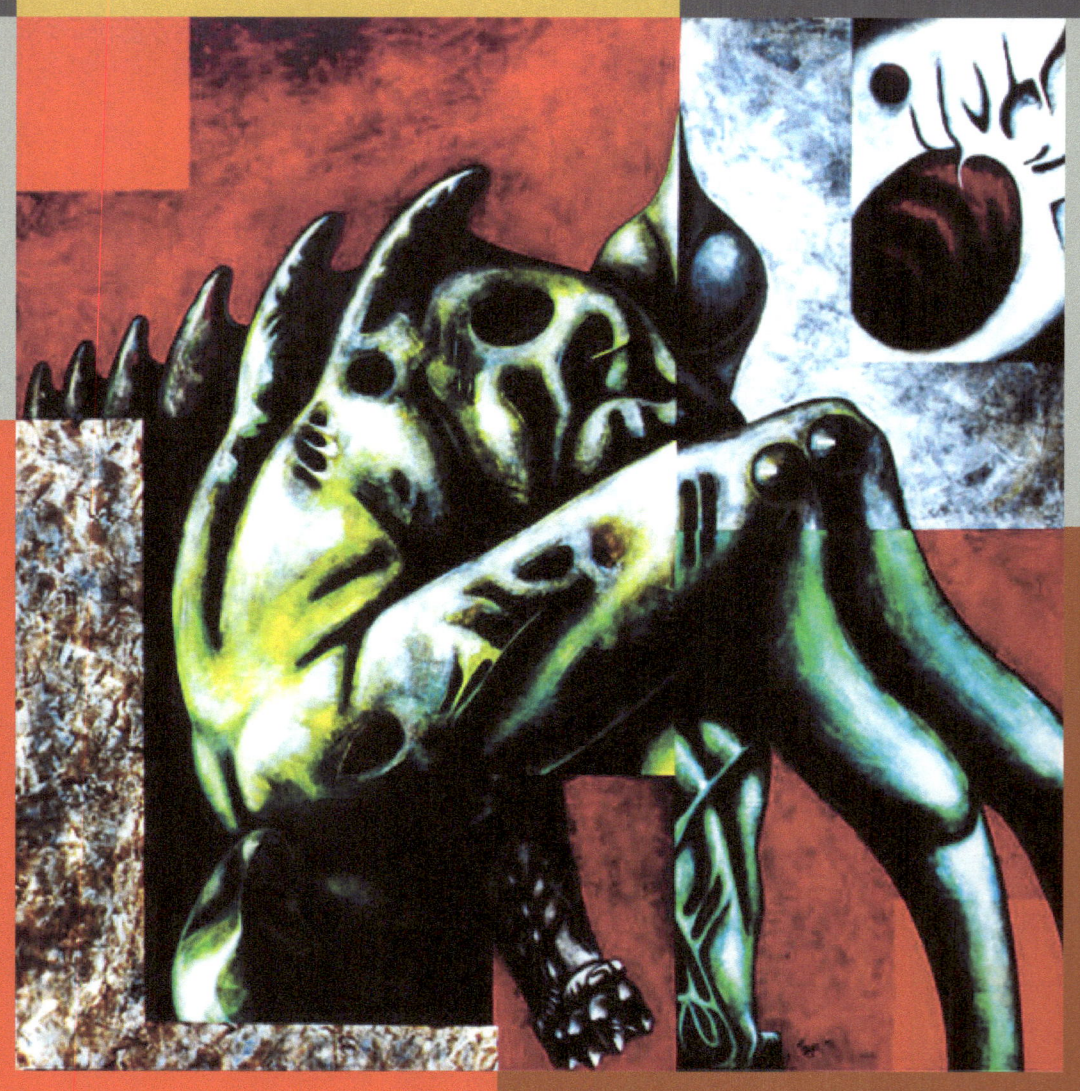

Homo-ortóptero
Enamel / Wood Panel
150 cm x 150 cm
1998

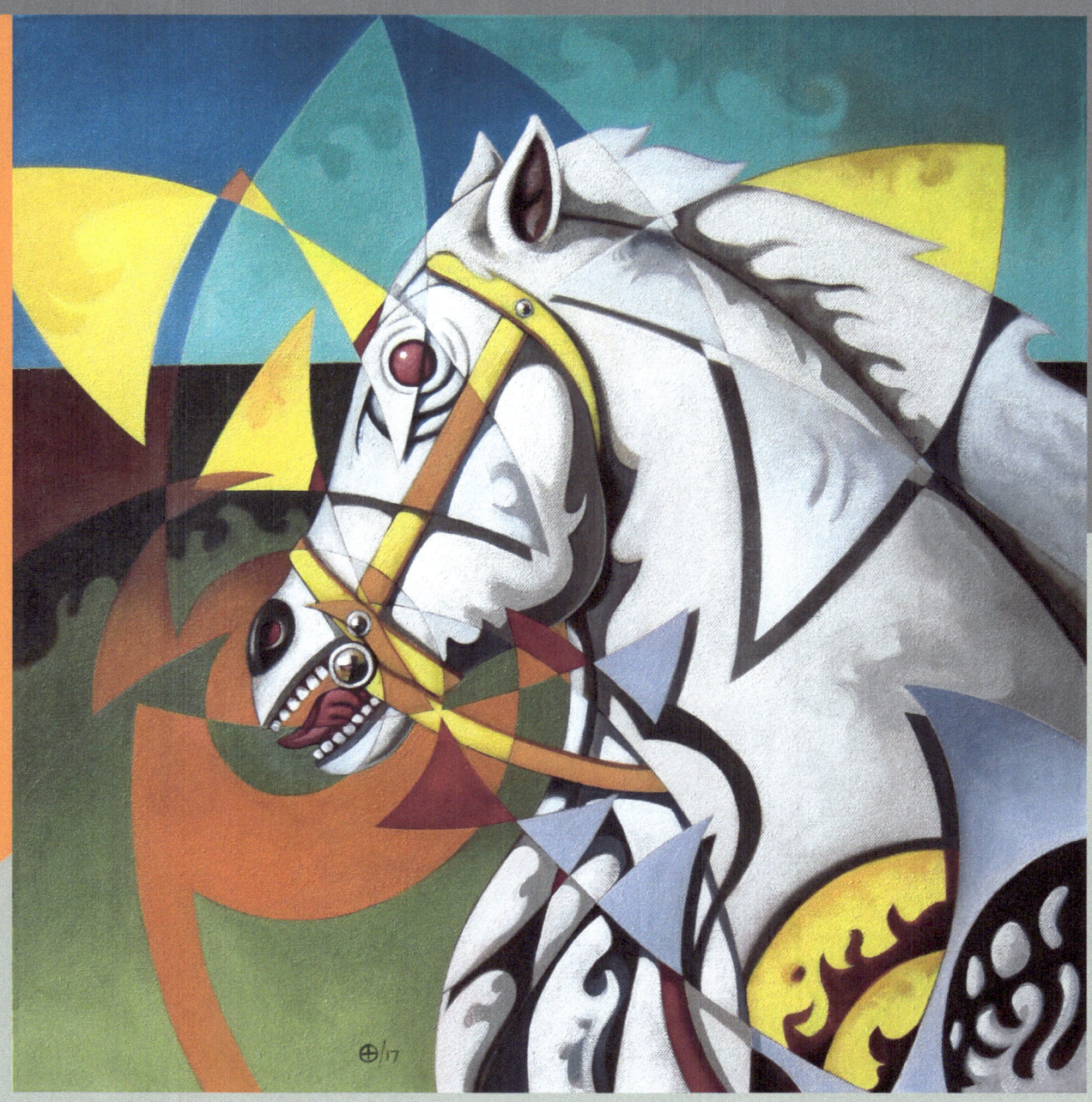

Caballo en fuga
Oil / Canvas
60 cm x 60 cm
2017

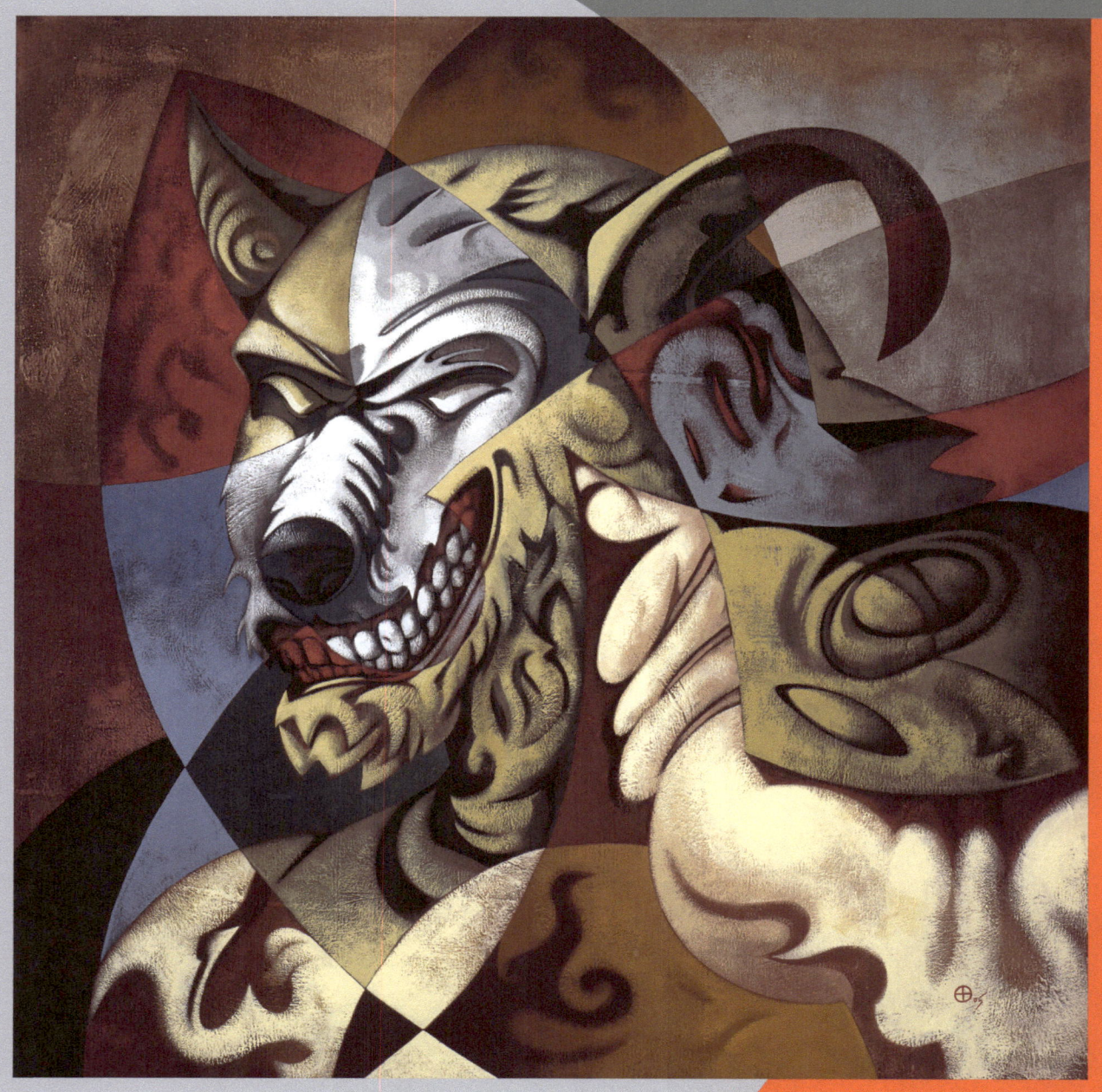

Hemofiction dog
Enamel / Canvas
35" x 36"
2005

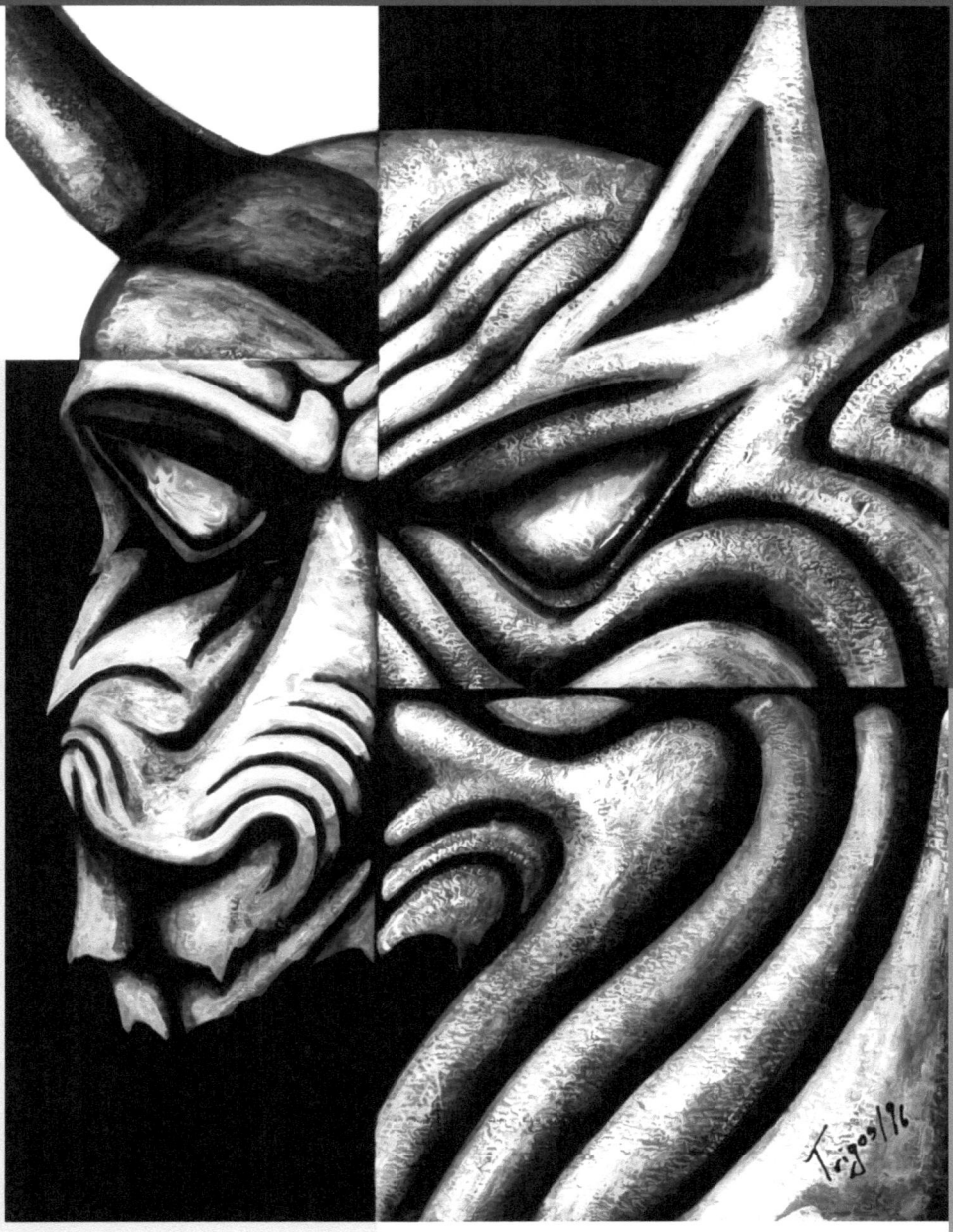

Chorrillo
Acrylic / Cardboard
25 cm x 20cm
1996

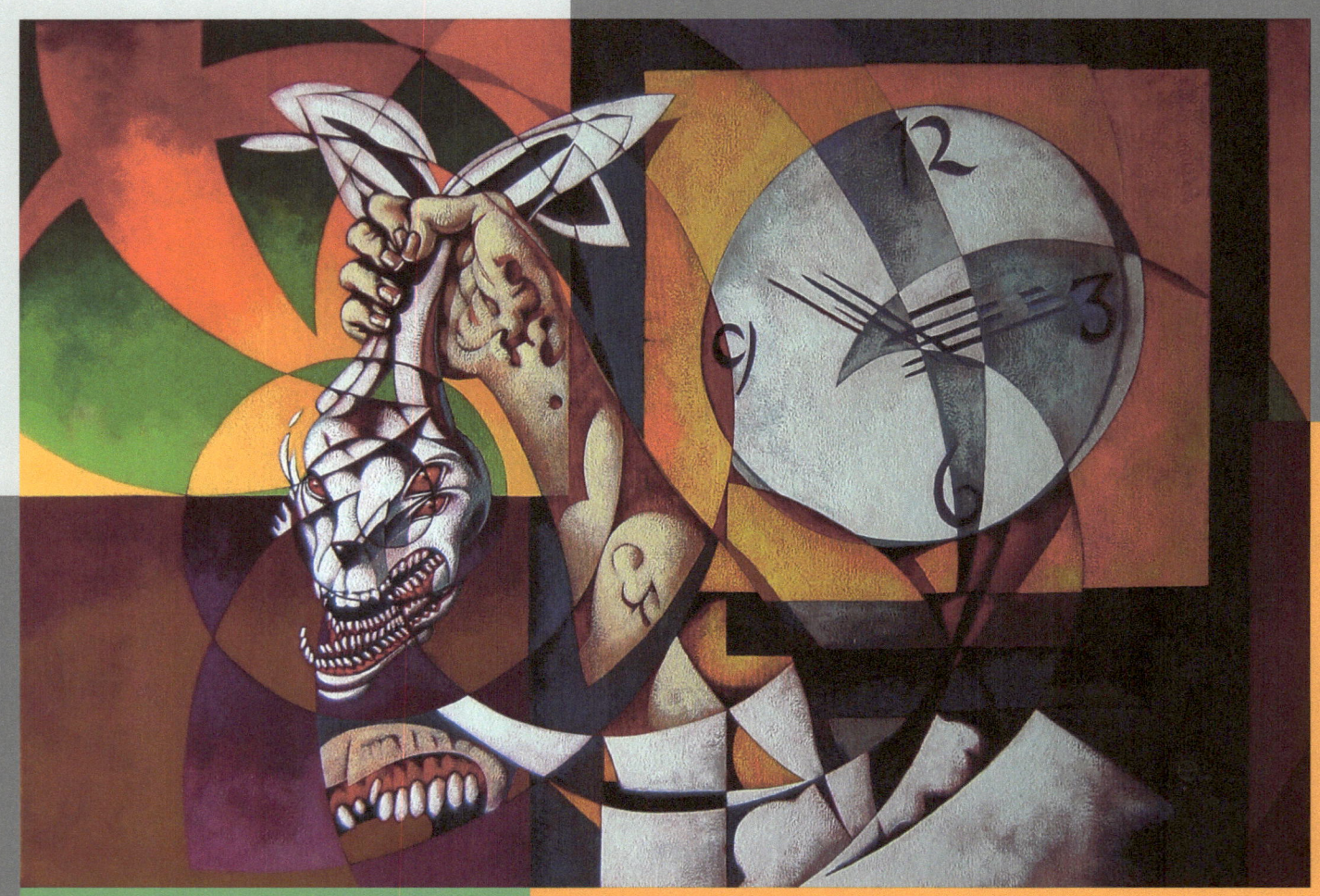

Hemofiction rabbit
Enamel / Canvas
24" x 36"
2009

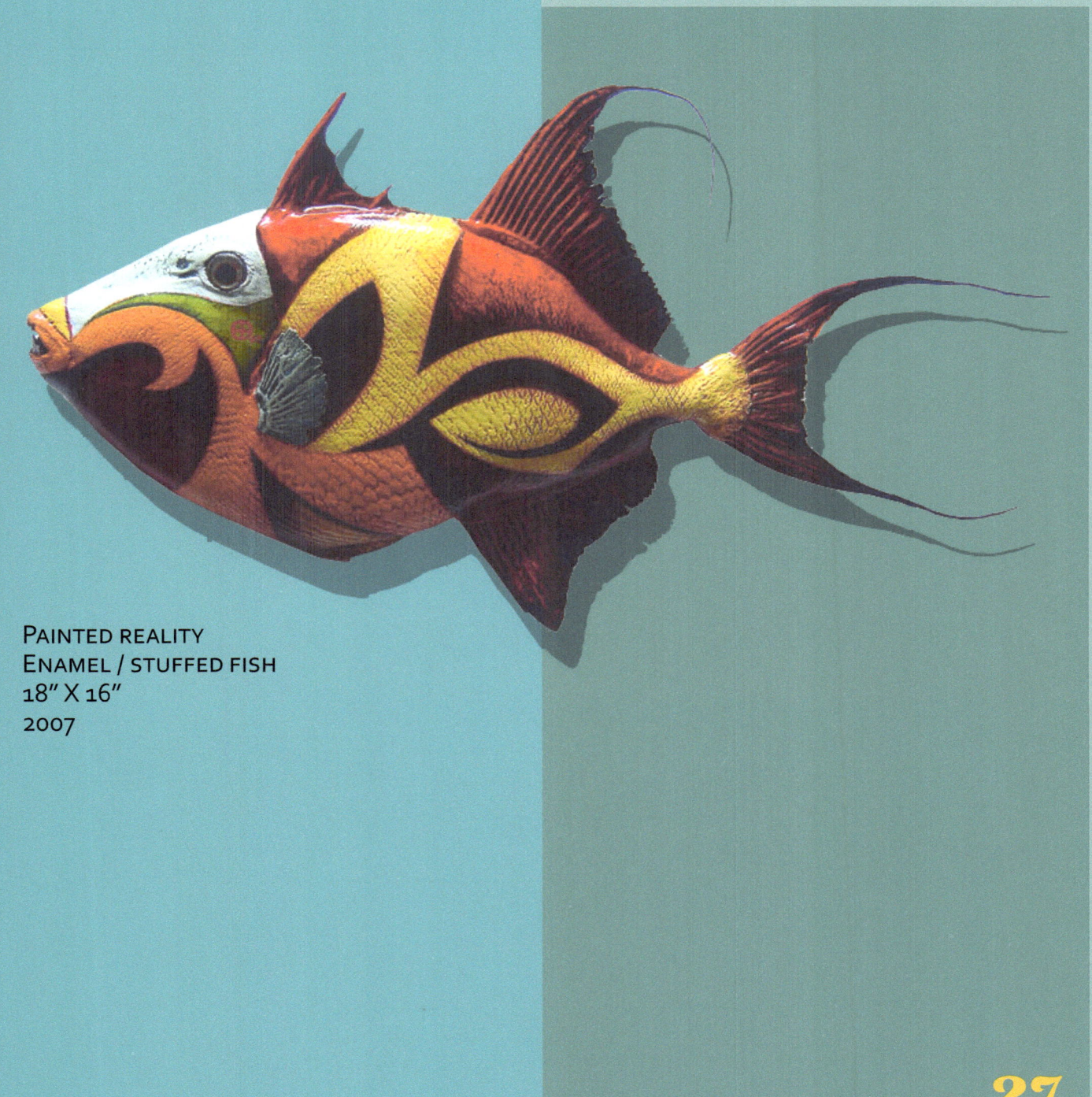

Painted reality
Enamel / stuffed fish
18" x 16"
2007

27

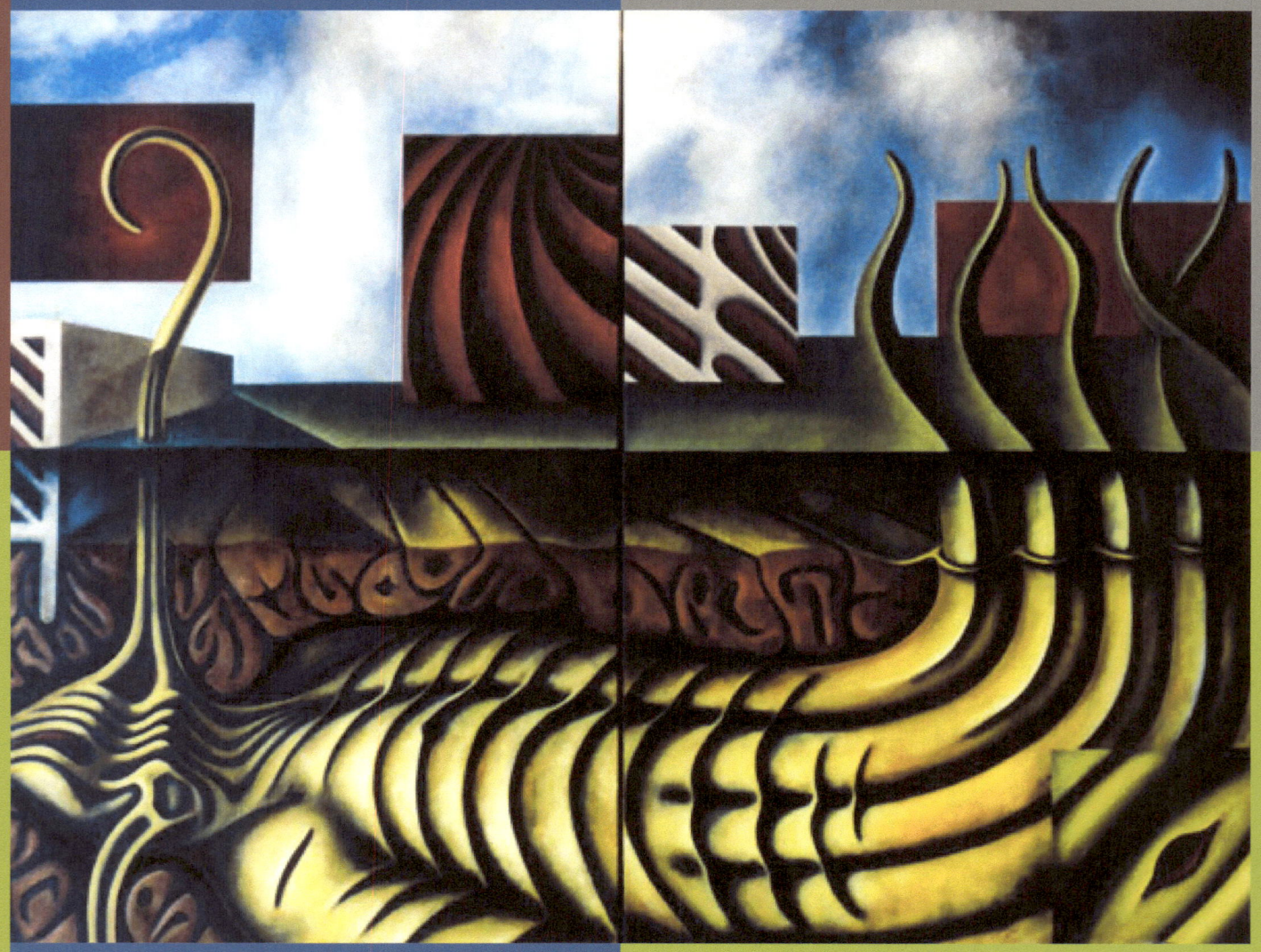

Vegetación humana
oil / Canvas
150 cm X 200 cm
1995